Bleeding Beauty

Lucy Radcliffe

India | USA | UK

Bleeding Beauty © 2024 Lucy Radcliffe

All rights reserved.

No part of this publication may be reproduced, stored in a retrieval system, or transmitted, in any form or by any means, electronic, mechanical, photocopying, recording or otherwise, without the prior written permission of the presenters.

Lucy Radcliffe asserts the moral right to be identified as author of this work.

Presentation by *BookLeaf Publishing*

Web: www.bookleafpub.com

E-mail: info@bookleafpub.com

ISBN: 9789358319859

First edition 2024

For my mamai

who raised and reared me into the woman I am today

ACKNOWLEDGEMENT

I would like to express my deepest gratitude to the McCourt Sisters for answering all my burning questions.
To my siblings who made me the happiest big sister in the world.
To my parents who I am eternally grateful for, their support has been immense.
To my grandparents who have shown me what true love is.
To my partner who I've forced to read every single line of my work, thank you, I love you more than you know.
To Maya Angelou who gave me my love of poetry.
To all the women who made my girlhood memorable; Carrágh, Ella, Cara, Sarah and Sami.
To all the menstruating people reading this for allowing me to share our mutual experiences of this world.

PREFACE

This book is an exploration of my personal experiences living and growing as a girl, a woman, a sister and a mother in the years to come. The deep desire to pick apart and portray the threads of this warm blanket of femininity I wrap around myself was unmeasurable. I felt a strong impulse to illustrate female anatomy, to show the pain and violence it endures while also capturing its strength and marvel.

These encounters throughout life are unique to individuals with cycles that mimic our constellations. It was very healing and liberating to write, I hope it reads that way too.

Biological Clock

I blew out my candles
and I made a wish.
I wished to be older.

In autumn, I bloom,
full breasts, round hips,
a bloodied womb,
plump skin, plump lips.
Only twelve and gazes loomed,
I grew accustomed to their stares,
or perhaps I was groomed not to care.

Smooth, glistening and new.
For you;
my cheeks glow and
my blood is thickening.
Spin me around,
take me in,
skin me,
tear me limb from limb.
Do what you want,
leave me gaunt,
or put me on your arm to flaunt.
You thieve my youth.

I blew out my candles
and I made a wish.
I wished to be younger.

Twenty and my time runs fine.
Where is my validation?
Does my skin no longer shine?
Is there not enough of me to ration?
Where is the line of slow men?
Have I gone out of fashion?

Tell me, when did I grow too old.

When I saw the red dot, my heart sank.
I became an object to be bled and led,
my desirability was sought after for some time.
I was to be wed, bred and then dead,
for what am I without my fertility?
I'm nothing without my red dot, without my hymen.
But my body betrays me,
for I rot as I ripen.

Sister

Our hearts beat as one,
from the moment I met you
with your tiny hands and feet
I knew this love was true.

Strawberry blonde
smiling big and still growing
Does she too feel this bond?
I pave the way into the unknown,
and then beyond.
but will it be enough?
My beautiful girl,
I want to do my best by you
life can be a whirl
how can I shield you
this world is too tough
for us.

Stay a little lady
there's no need to rush
it's overrated baby,
periods, creeps and thrush
just stay a little lady;
and maybe
I'll be able to keep you safe,
bundled up in our pillow fort estate.

Girl's Bathroom

A weighted walk,
head pounding
I don't know how anyone else can talk,
dark and dingy surroundings
this hallway is too long
but behind that door a world is unlocked.

Holding back hair,
sharing lipsticks,
most come in pairs
but here everyone's synergistic.
Familiar strangers,
we become one.
angels fix wardrobe malfunctions
"You're as beautiful as the sun"
- optimistic introductions.

On the walls,
in the stalls,
old and new scriptures
paint a picture
preserving memories of nights before
of course we add more.
Our names join them;
the girl's bathroom, an artistic gem.

My Lady

Those lips of wine
stain my skin
her touch, so divine,
she holds my chin
whispering, "all mine".
it almost feels like a sin
but that grin, it shines
how can I deny this fire within?

For your attention, your eye,
oh baby for you I'd burn
hooked on your love, I'm high
to be your joy, that's what I yearn
you're a lady and I'm just a boy.

Kiss me,
hold me,
you are sweet bliss,
your hair of gold,
with you, nothing is amiss
with you, I'd grow old.

The Pill

Tender breasts
No menstruation
Organs feel like they're rearranging
Larger breasts
Always fatigued
Again, my body is changing

Constant thirst
Weight gain
It's a sacrifice I make
No sex drive
Too horny
So we don't have a small mistake

Bloated
Overly emotional
Can't wait for my prescription to end
Stretch marks
Random cramping
Then I'll be me again

Bouquet

I began my bloom with carnations;
rounded and petite, young and new.
Finally here after all my manifestations,
the rest was still nestled safely in its bud
with nourishment, my garden grew
whispering grass soon stained by blood.

Lilies of the valley I now hold to my chest,
tear dropped and marked with growth.
Soft to the touch, my beautiful breasts
crafted by my body, a breathtaking bouquet
for them, how had I once held such loath
they display grace like no other, I'd say.

Girlhood With You

I close my eyes and I see all of you; young and new
huddled around lunch tables gossiping, cackling.
The girls who I grew with, the women I now view.
Periods, DIY tutorials, makeup tips and boys
conversations unravelling, in my eyes you were all dazzling
oh how I miss this - your joy, your voice, the noise
of our childhoods.

I wonder if you too see our reflections within my smile
for I see little you, hidden beneath the memory rich
lines that frame your face. Even if its been a while
I hope you know the love I hold for you, girl.
You've got a place in my heart and soul, which
is all for you. One day we'll rule this world,
just me and you.

Thank you for giving me a girlhood one could only dream for -

Carrágh, Ella, Cara, Eimear, Sarah, Sami

Oldest of, Oldest of, Oldest

One
The first
Where it all begun
Taken from the mother
Not once nursed
Given to another.

Haunted by the spirit
Heal it with the eucharist
Was this all inherited?
Clerical collars turn away
So we turn on Christ
I curse them to this day.

Our Lady,
Abandoned by her God,
Born of a mothers sacrifice
The rage it caused
Will the suffering suffice,
Will they call us crazy?

———————

The daughter
Wrapped in white
Doused with blessed water
Her fathers delight,
A girl of magic
a mind so bright
A tale so tragic

The curse of Eve,
She does it alone
The path, she will weave
that will of stone

won't let her grieve
She stands in the unknown
Begging no-one else to leave.

Woman of rib,
Abandoned by her God,
Made into a she-devil
The rage it caused
She would show them true evil,
Through her crib.

Born of the earthly dust
With a bite of venom
Learnt to live without trust
Burnt by desperate men
They try again, she won't let 'em
Instead shunning them with pen.

Oldest of, oldest of, oldest,
Unbent and discontent, housing all the rage,
Boldest and coldest, their violence she noticed
She banishes them from the garden
With their behaviour put on stage
Generations of hearts hardened,
Her temper is her heritage.

Sweet Lilit,
The lord, she no longer obeys
Serpent hisses with aggression
Each day she makes him pay
She does it for her succession
In hopes to heal the spirit.

Mothers Closet

Draping dress, beetling blazer, oversized heels,
unsteady on my feet, red on my smiling teeth
dressed in her Sunday Best, how'd that make her feel
I complain about the drooping bust - I haven't got the breasts
I haven't got the hips, won't have them till my eighteenth
I haven't had my first bra yet, she says; "you're still in vests -
princess," and she's right. Mamaí is always right.
I want to be a beautiful girl, like the girl and pearl
For that I need to be higher in height and remain polite
for that I need an ass and I want a big bosom,
gotta lose the vest, get into bras. I give her a twirl.
She calls me pretty; maybe I would be, if I was a woman
And not a little girl.

I steal a low cut top - filling out the bust with my tits
Mamaí says it served her well, but it's mine now
surprised that it fits, on my curves it perfectly sits
each time I vow is the last then I find myself inside again
she always allows me at her collections; lets me to chow
Down. She says "you're a ten" and I say "you bet I am - amen".
Mamaí looks at me with those eyes of loving sorrow,
a look of longing: searching for the girl hidden beneath my shadow,
maybe she'll appear in the morrow, but the chances are narrow
she stares at me and looking back is the woman she watered
deep below the girl we both know, still hoping to grow
it is both she and I that her sight sought; if only I could have offered
a look at her little girl.

Possession

to be used,
endure pain,
remain pure,
have a brain,
but stay in your lane,
and don't you dare complain,
be confident
but not vain,
grow the seed
do it again
bleed and breed
All for the men.

My voice carries the screams of generations
The bitterness runs raw in the famous throng
Of women. Sick of the same regulations
Forced upon our bodies. This is my fertile land
Not yours. Let us sing our sorrowful song
He won't understand, it'll all go as planned
He won't question till we bring forth our aggression
Hysterical women, annoying bitches, stupid sluts - Fuck YOU
No longer under oppression; no longer your possession
We the sirens, witches and bitches, we become what you view as
taboo.

Birth

Squatting deep,
rocking on my heels,
desperate for sleep,
Through the hall, joy sweeps.
But I weep;
for soon we will separate
and you will be your own.

Born from my blood,
pushing for perfection,
you are so beloved.
Waxy white mush hugs you,
the last layer of protection
I provide for your debut.

The butterflies of meeting someone new
mix with the gore and sweat
But i come to find,
it's a face of someone I already knew
someone i already met.

We take our first breaths together;
we cry out for each other
Your skin of delicate feather,
Your eyes, a squinted mirror
The birth of a mother
Entering the world through her,
With her - endear her.

Childhood Bedroom

I mourn the little girl I grew from
but I still find her in places
traces linger in familiar spaces
does she think of who we've become?

She is the withering stickers that ferment
on my bed frames.
She is the chipping paint on cement
pink underneath proclaims
her memories extent.
I feel her when I cuddle our teddy bear,
even after twenty years.
I feel her when I collect a doll thats rare,
a glee that never disappears
in a way, she's still there.

I'm still the girl I always was,
still swinging, skipping and singing.
Shopping, spinning and springing.
I do it 'cause I can, I do it just 'cause.

Of The Sorrows

Beautifully born by prophecy of a man,
not of a god, it cemented as a curse.
Her hand sold, accepted by the clan.
Hidden away till she'd bleed,
her heart he would coerce,
he'd make her grow his seed.
Her misery was to be spared
as a babe, her life was to be freed.
The lust of a king claimed her instead.
beautifully born to breed his greed.

Before he can stain her youth
she marries in secret; for love.
The king is enraged at the truth
off they run; safety within reach.
Tricked with the idea of the dove
their shield of joy the king will breach;
murdered before her young eyes
widowed, her sorrow the king will leach.
Her cries burn as he takes his prize.
Kept for a year on his tight leash.

Her voice was silenced,
her agency was stolen,
her life meets its violent
end. Her beauty is broken.
by her own choice she
takes her last breath; she regains her voice.

Mirror / Body

In my mirror I see my image
my hair, my eyes, my skin
most days, I grimace.
Red roots grow across breasts
bumps on hips, I cringe within.
It feels like a million tests,
if I'm strong and tough,
if I can call my own bluff,
If I love myself enough.

Summer Wine

I dream of your lips
Caressing my skin
Hands gripping hips
I beg for you to come in
Shadows of your fingertips
Dance across porcelain.
Your effect on me is lingering
Without you I feel I haven't eaten;
I'm not breathing,
Come back to the silk
For you, I am sweeten
We can sway in sync.

Nude
Fingers interlocked
Cravings are yet to be subdued
Your touch tickles down my thigh
Leave your mark,
My body begs; you comply.
Your tongue, on route
I express my need and you proceed
Digging deep into the grapefruit
My pleasure, I preach
You suck the pomegranate seed -
It is juicy like a peach

Arched back,
Curled toes
I feel exposed
I lay here unclothed, posed
You're also stripped to your own
With you, I feel a little less alone.

Mental Load

I have the ovaries,
I do the dishes,
I get the groceries,
I also cook,
I give out the magic kisses.
What tasks have you undertook?
Who plants the seed?
Who waters the crop?
Why must I plead,
I wish we could swap,
if only for a day.
My career is a consequence,
what about your false incompetence?
A house I built,
yet I'm the one with guilt?

My Rock

Mother is my rock,
first best friend,
quayside walks,
a shoulder to depend.

Hair of fire,
eyes of ocean,
a bit of a crier,
with plenty of emotion.

Her first born,
aren't I blessed?
She's seen my worst,
but created my best.

My heart, she crafted,
with care,
i'd love to restart,
to hold her heart
and take away her future despair.

Give me her pain,
contain it, put it on me,
oh lord,
it's the least I owe.
Turn back the clock,
if only for my rock.

My Brother and Me

I have a brother
that I love so much.

I poured his cereal, I paired his socks, I taught him all I know.
He has my humour, he has my smile, he has my voice.
No longer the little boy I raised; each day I watch him grow.
I wonder if he remembers the lessons his sister taught,
Of womanhood, of menstruation, of consent and choice.
If his mind is tainted by those men, I'll be left distraught

I have a brother,

Who is now a young man. A memory of a toothless smile.
He's bigger now but not the oldest; I'll always be the shield.
Men I've met; hostile, vile. But for him, only the best I compile -
patience, kindness, understanding and as much love as I can
from those toxic ideals I keep him concealed,
preventing him from growing into a hurtful type of man.

I have a brother

I raised to be good and just.
Because I always want to defend him;
even if he breaks the trust,
so I rear him with this expectation
to have respect for our skin,
my duty of care is his education.

I have a brother
that I love so much.

My First Period

Twelve, a lotus bloom
our first encounter
in that small room
the day I met her
a monthly power
a lifetime together.

My river of red
it comes in a surge
it spreads with an invisible thread
digging and ripping my skin
bloody purge but my strengths emerge
soon she will again begin.

From girlhood to womanhood,
she's with me for a while
she's with me for good.
I'll accept her with a smile.

Weight of Life

The creases of my face show,
the emotions I have held.
The veins of my arms show,
the paths I have felled.
The liverspots of my skin show,
the places the sun kissed and held.
The greying of my roots show,
the ones I have lost and dwelled.

This is the face of mother nature,
who experienced a wide range
who has known great labour,
with age I embrace such change,
yet it feels so strange.

A reflection of a life well lived
a life I have survived,
a life I have thrived,
soon, the end will arrive.
But at least my skin will show I was alive,
that in love I was not deprived.

Dear Future Daughter

Dear future daughter,
oh how I've yearned for you, prayed for you
I've dreamed of your smile, your laughter.
They say don't rush but I'd jump in head first
I always knew I was waiting for you
to cradle you, to smell you, to quench your thirst.
I always knew I was waiting for a second line
when I lift the plastic stick, I'll be ecstatic.
What I'd do to have you now, to have you as mine
I'll wait for you, till your ready for this world my little love
some would say it's dramatic or erratic,
but for your arrival, I'll plead with all the gods above.

Run, dance, leap through the fields, flowers and fairies,
don't stop chasing dreams embedded within stars.
Oh my curious girl, pick the sweetened blueberries
I'll lift you above waves, hold you above the cloud
in a world of softness, I wish I could say it's ours
I stay on the moon, you go to Mars, make yourself proud.
I want to apologise, I want to warn, I want to prepare
but what good will it do but steal your childish wonder?
Breathe in the air, sweet girl, have no fear instead be aware.
I'll hug and hold and kiss and squeeze and beg for you to stay little
your memory forever etched within my womb; I'll shelter you
from the wind, rain and thunder
so stay with me, who has time for the confusing adolescent riddle.

Now you're a woman, phenomenally. Phenomenal woman,
that's who I raised. That's how I was raised.
Not by shy mothers, not by quiet mothers,
by dancing till nigh mothers, by riot till equity mothers.
Glancing back you'll see us; mothers of great complexity,
now don't you slack, feel our weight - hold our weight
you can bare it as we all have because you're a woman
of many phenomenal mothers.

Milton Keynes UK
Ingram Content Group UK Ltd.
UKHW030254190324
439698UK00015B/975